D0061777

ANDROMACHE

ALSO BY RICHARD WILBUR

A HARVEST/HBJ BOOK

HARCOURT BRACE JOVANOVICH, PUBLISHERS

SAN DIEGO   NEW YORK   LONDON

JEAN RACINE

ANDROMACHE

TRAGEDY IN FIVE ACTS, 1667

TRANSLATED INTO ENGLISH VERSE BY

RICHARD WILBUR

DRAWINGS BY IGOR TULIPANOV

Library of Congress Cataloging in Publication Data

Racine, Jean, 1639–1699.
Andromache: tragedy in five acts, 1667.

(A Harvest/HBJ book)
Translation of: Andromaque.
I. Wilbur, Richard, 1921–   . II. Title.
PQ1890.A38   1984   842'.4   83-18439

ISBN 0-15-607510-5

First Harvest/HBJ Edition 1984

B C D E

For Charlee

INTRODUCTION

Francis Fergusson, in his *The Idea of a Theater*, makes the best possible case for seeing Jean Racine as a master of the "theater of reason"—a kind of drama which implies a fixed society and which celebrates the triumph of heroic responsibility over the passions. Mr. Fergusson's main exhibit is *Berenice*, a play in which three royal persons painfully renounce their desires for duty's sake; and to such a play his terms may plausibly apply. But they do not in the least describe Racine's first great tragedy, *Andromache*, whose obsessed and driven principals are incapable of rising above themselves, and whose "world" implies a French society of crumbling values and superficial order.

What impels the action of *Andromache* is love; not affectionate and well-wishing love, but the kind of which La Rochefoucauld observed that, judging by its results, it is closer to hatred than to friendship. In Racine, such love is felt as a fatality which enslaves the lover's will, and blinds him to all but a fierce need to possess the beloved; it is a passion which, if rebuffed, may turn to enmity, and which in its reckless exorbitance seems to aim less at happiness than at self-destruction. The plot of *Andromache*, largely animated by this emotional formula, presents us from the first with a chain of obstructed passions: Orestes loves Hermione, who has once refused him; Hermione loves her fiancé, King Pyrrhus of Epirus; Pyrrhus loves his Trojan captive Andromache; Andromache loves her dead husband, Hector. What brings this frozen situation to a crisis, and resolves it in one day, is Orestes' arrival in Epirus as ambassador of the Greeks, demanding that Pyrrhus surrender Andromache's small son Astyanax, so that the Greeks may execute him and thus put an end to Hector's line. The Greek demand permits Pyrrhus to threaten the long-reluctant Andromache: unless she marries him, he will sacrifice her son. Andromache, whose nature is at once innocent and wily, responds with an apparent compliance, and from that decision all else follows: the wrath of the jilted Hermione, her demand that the infatuated Orestes avenge her, the death of two of the principals and the madness of a third.

This is not, then, a noble Cornelian play in which the characters subordinate passion to duty and honor; what happens is mostly ignoble, and is the result of the characters' subjection to love and hate. Orestes has accepted his embassy for false and private reasons, and ends "by breaking all the laws designed / By Heaven for monarchs, envoys, and mankind." Hermione speaks of honor but remains nonetheless in Epirus, permitting herself to be dishonored by Pyrrhus and invoking as pretext a duty which she does not feel. Pyrrhus brutally maltreats a highborn woman who is his captive and, in breaking his sworn word to Hermione, violates his alliance with the Greeks. Even Andromache, whose wifely and maternal loves may seem blameless, is reasonably judged by some scholars to be unheroic in her long refusal of Pyrrhus; proud of her royal lineage and of Troy, she yet declines, out of personal feeling, to return to the world of power in which she and Hector's son belong. Her "innocent stratagem" (Act IV, Scene 1) is in any case not admirable. It is only at rare and brief moments that the main characters are aware of the claims of reason and society, or direct their emotions toward any but those who are the objects of their obsessions. If Pyrrhus for a spell remembers his kingly responsibilities and turns toward Hermione, it is out of a temporary hatred for Andromache; Hermione wavers not between Pyrrhus and Orestes but between love and hate for Pyrrhus; Andromache thinks only of Hector, with whose image she has blended that of her son; and when Orestes expresses concern for the safety of his friend Pylades (Act III, Scene 1), it is only the most fleeting respite from his absorption with himself and with Hermione. The people of this play do not live in life's moral and political dimensions, where self-transcendence is possible; they are alone with their fatalities and fixations.

And yet the play continually evokes the aristocratic ideals which its characters violate. The speeches of old Phoenix, tutor both to Achilles and to his son Pyrrhus, are full of public virtue, advising self-mastery and prudent statesmanship. If the Trojan war is often depicted (by Andromache, Pyrrhus, Hermione) as a wretched slaughter, the recent past is also repeatedly recalled as a time of nobility, heroism, and magnanimity from which the present has fallen away. Andromache, exercising what a French critic has called "the coquetry of virtue," manipulates Pyrrhus by appealing to the man he knows he should be—greathearted, judicious, and principled. Orestes speaks the language of gallantry, and is chivalrously quick to answer his lady's demand for vengeance; when that vengeance turns out to be a cowardly assassination, he has a clear and agonized awareness of the moral and social laws which he has broken. Finally, the stage-set is a room in a palace, and the stage is full of Milords, Miladies, and all those formalities which belong to the highest level of a stable and glorious social order.

Which brings me to the question of how Racine, and this play in particular, ought to be translated into English. There are good reasons for not trying to duplicate in our tongue the rhymed couplets of French tragedy. For one thing, our audiences are better prepared to accept rhymed verse in comedy than in tragedy. For another, rhyme is rather less emphatic in French than in the strongly stressed English tongue, and a rhymed Racine play in English is therefore in danger of seeming more self-conscious than the original—more a dramatic poem for various voices than the passionate speeches of distinct characters. That would be unfortunate. On the other hand, there are good and even compelling reasons for taking the risk of rhyming. Racine's language is always simple and powerful, but it operates on more than one level of diction. W. G. Moore tells us that Racine was one of the "modernising playwrights" of the French seventeenth century who invigorated the old declamatory drama by introducing "the natural alongside the elevated." If one is going to parallel such juxtapositions of the heightened and the plain as we find at the opening of Act IV, Scene 3, the flatness of blank verse will not do; one needs the full music of rhyme to make the contrast strong and at the same time to bind it into the flow of the dialogue. It might also be argued that the repetitions of rhyme contribute, in a play like *Andromache*, to the atmosphere of obsession. But the best justification I have found lies in a sentence of Martin Turnell's. The originality of Racine's drama, he says, consists "in the contrast between extreme violence and the tightness of the form, between the primitive passions simmering just below the surface of civilized society and the versification which reflects the outer shape of that society." The form is part of the meaning, then, and I have tried, by putting Racine's rhymed alexandrines into English couplets, to render that dimension fully.

Andromache is written within a very narrow vocabulary, and incessantly repeats in fresh conjunctions such key words as *destin, courroux, yeux, feu, cruel, ingrat, funeste.* Though the multiple demands of translation have sometimes obliged me to use more synonyms than the original does, I have sought to keep close to Racine in this respect, since the repeated terms make for thematic emphasis and for comparison or contrast between speech and speech, scene and scene. I have deviated from Racine's rhyming practice in one way only: where he sees no harm, for example, in using the rhyme *douleurs / pleurs* twice within ten lines, I have avoided that sort of proximity in deference to present-day English-American taste, and out of a feeling that rhyme, in a tragic play, should in no way call attention to itself. In language, I have aimed at the transparent and undated; if any reader or hearer finds "'twas" or "'twixt" antique, I can only say that those words are regularly used in conversation by my Massachusetts townspeople.

It is frequently said that Racine is untranslatable, and that he is in any case not for export. Few English attempts upon Racine have been so well received as Ambrose Philips' *The Distrest Mother*, a free blank-verse adaptation of *Andromache* first acted in 1712. Adjusting *Andromache* to the English theater and sensibility, Philips broke up the longer speeches with interpolations or divided them between speakers, softened or sentimentalized the characters, and closed with a heartwarming reunion between Andromache and her child. Thus skillfully doctored, the play had a long history of productions, though it still did not please everyone; Leigh Hunt exploded, after seeing it, that it was "French all over . . . pompous, frigid, and ranting." The fact is that Racine's theater is not ours, and that it is usually described by us in terms of its exclusions. The *Times* recently quoted an art critic as saying that "in Racine, nobody sneezes; the disorder of everyday life is outlawed by classic tradition." True enough. Racine's drama is sparing of physical action; there is no dueling or dying onstage, no crowd movement, certainly no sneezing; there is but a single set, and what takes place on it, however dreadful, is contained by a courtly decorum; the characters speak—sometimes at length, and often in conventional dialogues between principal and confidant—within the artifice of rhyming verse. All this is so remote from our contemporary stage that "adaptation" could not possibly bring it near. Our best hope, I think, is to see whether a maximum fidelity, in text and in performance, might not adapt us to *it*.

What we have in *Andromache* is not "the disorder of everyday life" but a paroxysm of psychological violence; not for the sake of the classical "unities," but for the sake of displaying the passions under maximum pressure, Racine brings his characters together on the one day when all is to be decided. Their speeches, delivered in one room of Pyrrhus' palace, glance back at Troy or Sparta, at a past which has determined them and against which they are measured; their words also gradually create another location outside the palace—the temple, that place of marriage and of bloody sacrifice toward which their decisions are converging. But the focus is all on a confined and feverish here-and-now in which the principals waver, threaten, accuse, entreat, exploit, extenuate, feign, plot, deceive, and arrive at their terrible choices. The language in which this happens has, whatever Racine's detractors may say, none of the diffuseness of aria or of pompous oratory; the characters address their predicaments, or each other, in a spare, clear style which is often, as Lytton Strachey says, "compact as dynamite." It is a measure of Racine's economy and swiftness that Hermione, in Act II, Scene I, can credibly pass in some thirty lines through six shifts of attitude toward Pyrrhus. There is almost no soliloquy in the play, and as John C. Lapp has so well argued of Racine's drama as a whole, the characters engage, with the wary alertness of courtiers, in continual interaction. They observe each other closely; they dissimulate, or advise each other to do so; they react acutely not only to words but also to expressions, demeanors, hesitations, silences. Given this constant, intense, and articulate commerce between Racine's characters, it is all the more dramatic when one of them is reduced by conflict to incoherence (as Orestes is in Act II, Scene 4), or breaks the fabric of colloquy with a *non sequitur* (as Hermione does in the penultimate speech of Act II, Scene I.) *Andromache* is, in short, supremely a play of *inter*play, and I urge those who may perform this translation not to recite it, not to declaim it, but to act it.

I must thank Alex Szgoyi for giving me a copy of *Andromaque* some twenty years ago, and suggesting that I translate it. For one clarification or another, I am indebted to many scholars, commentators, and previous translators.

[*Introduction*]

And I am deeply grateful to James Merrill, Sonja and William Jay Smith, Lawrence Joseph, David Ball, my wife, and my son Nathan, for their criticism and encouragement.

Richard Wilbur

Cummington, Massachusetts
1981

ANDROMACHE

CHARACTERS

ANDROMACHE, Hector's widow, captive of Pyrrhus

PYRRHUS, Achilles' son, King of Epirus

ORESTES, Agamemnon's son

HERMIONE, Helen's daughter, betrothed to Pyrrhus

PYLADES, friend of Orestes

CLEONE, Hermione's confidante

CEPHISA, Andromache's confidante

PHOENIX, tutor of Achilles and, later, of Pyrrhus

ORESTES' RETINUE

The scene is at Buthrotum, a town in Epirus, in a chamber of Pyrrhus' palace.

First performed, in December of 1981, at the University of Maryland, Baltimore County, under the direction of Xerxes Mehta.

SCENE ONE

ORESTES, PYLADES

ORESTES

Yes, reunited with so true a friend,
I think my destiny shall soon amend;
Harsh fortune seems already less severe
Because she's brought about our meeting here.
How strange that, landing on this bitter shore,
Orestes should find Pylades once more,
Who, six months lost to me without report,
Is now restored to me at Pyrrhus' court!

PYLADES

For that, thank Heaven—whose tempests without cease
Have barred me from the sea-roads back to Greece
Since that bad day when heavy seas and gales
Just off Epirus, drove apart our sails.
During this exile, how I've been prey to fears
For you, how often given way to tears,
Conceiving some fresh danger you must bear
And which my truant friendship could not share!
Above all have I feared the black, depressed
Mood which so long has occupied your breast,
Fearing as well that Heaven, harshly kind,
Might grant the death you've sought so long to find.
But here you are, Sir, in Epirus, and
Clearly no dark fate brings you to this land:

7

The dazzling retinue you're followed by
Is not the train of one who seeks to die.

ORESTES

Ah, well. Fate leads me on, no telling whither.
Love for a heartless woman brings me hither,
But who knows how that god will cast my lot,
And whether I have come to die or not?

PYLADES

What! Shall you be Love's galley slave, and let
Him plot the course of your existence yet?
What spell has caused you to forget the pains
He's brought you, and once more to wear his chains?
D'you think Hermione, who was so unkind
In Sparta, will in Epirus change her mind?
Ashamed of all your fruitless pleas, you came
To hate her once, and would not speak her name.
Sir, you deceived me.

ORESTES

                    I was deceived, I fear.
Dear friend, don't chide a wretch who holds you dear.
When have I hid from you my heart's desires?
You saw my passion's birth, its earliest fires.
When Menelaus pledged his daughter as spouse
To Pyrrhus, the avenger of his house,
You saw my grief, and since have witnessed me
Dragging my chain of woes from sea to sea.
Against my will you followed everywhere
Your sad Orestes, pitying my despair,
And daily saved me, daily calmed the surge
Of some quick rage or self-destroying urge.
At last, reflecting how Hermione

8

Had turned her wiles toward Pyrrhus, scorning me,
My vengeful heart resolved, as you recall,
To blot her from my memory, once for all.
I thought, and others thought, that I was cured;
My fits were fits of hate, I felt assured.
I cursed her pride, I mocked her charms, I swore
Those eyes of hers would trouble me no more,
And thus I felt I'd set my heart at peace.
In that delusive calm I came to Greece,
And found its kings and princes all assembled
To cope with some great threat at which they trembled.
I joined them, sure that war and things of state
Would fill my thought with cares of greater weight;
That, roused once more to action, I would find
Love's final traces banished from my mind.
But look, my friend, how fate has made me run
Into the very snare I sought to shun.
The talk was all of Pyrrhus; on every side
The Greeks deplored a king who in his pride,
Forgetful of his blood and fealty,
Rears at his court all Hellas' enemy,
Astyanax, Hector's young and luckless boy,
Sole remnant of the buried kings of Troy.
Andromache, they told me, had beguiled
The sly Ulysses, so as to save her child:
Another infant, torn from her embrace,
Was thought her son, and slaughtered in his place.
Pyrrhus, they said, has shunned Hermione, and
Prefers another for his crown and hand;
Old Menelaus, though doubting what he heard,
Was grieved by wedding rites so long deferred.
The very anguish that his words expressed
Wakened a secret pleasure in my breast.
My heart leapt up; I told myself at first
That vengeful joy was all my spirit nursed.
But then I felt her cruel power revive;
My ill-extinguished fires were yet alive;

9

I knew that soon my hate would be no more,
Or, rather, that I loved her as before.
Thus I besought the Greeks to make of me
Their messenger to Pyrrhus; and, as you see,
I've come to tear from his protecting arm
A child whose life fills nations with alarm—
Though gladly would I let the boy remain,
Could I but steal my princess back again!
Don't dream that any peril could dismay
The twice-born passion that I feel today;
Having in vain opposed my destiny,
I blindly yield my will to its decree.
I love Hermione, and am here to try
To win her, to abduct her, or to die.
You who know Pyrrhus, tell me, where does he stand?
What's happening in his heart, his court, his land?
Is he still bound to my Hermione,
Or will he, Pylades, give her back to me?

PYLADES

If I dared promise that she'll be restored
To you by Pyrrhus, I should speak false, my lord.
Not that he seems enamored of his prize;
It's Hector's widow who fills his heart and eyes.
He loves her; but that widow has, to date,
Only repaid his love with stubborn hate;
To which the king responds by daily trying
Either to woo her or be terrifying.
He hides her son from her, brings her to tears
With threats to kill him, then allays her fears.
A hundred times Hermione's seen her lover
Return enraged to vow his worship of her
And offer at her feet, in dedication,
Sighs prompted less by love than by frustration.
Thus you may see, Sir, that one cannot say

What his vexed heart will do from day to day.
He might, my lord, in these distracted states,
Harm what he loves and marry what he hates.

ORESTES

But tell me, is Hermione not pained—
Her marriage thus delayed, her charms disdained?

PYLADES

Outwardly, Sir, Hermione has borne
Her fiancé's inconstancy with scorn;
She says he'll soon creep back to her, and plead
That her proud heart take pity on his need.
But I've been privy to her tears, my lord;
She weeps in secret to see her charms ignored;
She vows to leave, but lingers all the same,
And calls at times upon Orestes' name.

ORESTES

Ah, Pylades, if she had need of me,
I'd hasten—

PYLADES

            Sir, first discharge your embassy.
Inform the king that all the Greeks as one
Are leagued in enmity toward Hector's son.
Far from acceding, he will hold more dear
The woman whom he loves, the child they fear—
A pair your pleas and threats will not divide.
Press your demands, Sir! They shall be denied.
Here's Pyrrhus.

[*Act One* · *Scene One*]

ORESTES

Then go; prepare my torturer
For one whose only mission is to her.

SCENE TWO

ORESTES

Before the Greeks address you through my voice,
Let me declare my pleasure in their choice
Of envoy, Sir, whereby I see with joy
Achilles' son, the vanquisher of Troy.
Your deeds have matched your father's, in our view.
Great Hector fell by him, and Troy by you.
Achilles' place, as you have bravely shown,
Could have been claimed but by his son alone.
But he would not, like you, to Hellas' pain,
Nurture the blood of ruined Troy again
By yielding to a dangerous pity for
The sole survivor of so long a war.
Have you forgot what Hector was, my lord?
Our weakened peoples well recall his sword.
Widows and daughters tremble at his name;
No family in Hellas but can claim
From his ill-fated son a debt long due
For husbands and for fathers Hector slew.
And who knows what this son may some day dare?
Perhaps we'll see him raid our ports, and there
Set all our ships aflame, and like his sire
Pursue them out to sea with sword and fire.
May I express my heartfelt counsel, Sir?
Fear what reward your kindness may incur;
Take care, Sir, lest this bosom serpent give

You fatal thanks for having let him live.
Do then as all the Greeks would have you do;
Assure your vengeance, and your safety too;
Destroy this foe, this double threat to peace
Who'll try his strength on you, then war on Greece.

PYRRHUS

Greece need not be so anxious for my sake:
I'd thought that graver matters were at stake,
And, given the fame of her ambassador,
I judged some noble project was in store.
Who'd think so poor an errand could be run
By you, my lord, by Agamemnon's son;
That Greece, upon whom victory has so smiled,
Would stoop to plot the killing of a child?
Am I to sacrifice him? At whose demand?
Does Greece still hold his life within her hand?
Am I the sole Greek captain who may not
Dispose of captives who are his by lot?
Yes, Prince, beneath Troy's smoking walls, when we
Blood-spattered victors shared by lottery
The spoils of war, as all agreed to do,
It was Andromache and her son I drew.
Sad Hecuba to Ulysses' ship was sent;
To Argos, with your sire, Cassandra went;
Have I contested any of their shares,
Or claimed the slaves that rightfully were theirs?
Hector and Troy will rise again, they say:
His son, if spared, will murder me some day.
My lord, I think that an excessive dread.
I can't imagine ills so far ahead.
I bring to mind that city before her fall,
Her heroes many, and her ramparts tall,
Mistress of Asia; and I also see
What Troy's fate was, and what her fate must be.
I see but ruined towers which ashes cover,

Deserted meadowlands, a bloodstained river,
A child in chains; shall Troy in such a state
Hope to recover and retaliate?
Come, now! If Hector's son was meant to die,
Why have we spared him one whole year, and why
Was he not put to death on Priam's breast,
And buried under Troy with all the rest?
Then all seemed just. Old age and childhood pled
That they were helpless, and were stricken dead.
Darkness and victory, more cruel than we,
Incited us to random butchery.
Enraged, I slew all Troy that crossed my path.
But shall my cruelty outlast my wrath?
And shall I with deliberate calm ignore
My pity, and bathe my hands in infant gore?
No, Prince; let Greece seek other prey, and chase
Troy's sorry remnant in some other place.
My rage is spent, my vengeance at an end.
What Troy has saved, Epirus will defend.

ORESTES

My lord, you know too well through what a sly
Deceit a false Astyanax came to die,
As Hector's son had been condemned to do.
Not Troy but Hector is what the Greeks pursue.
They seek his son as payment for the guilt
Of Hector, who by all the blood he spilt
Begot a wrath his blood alone can sate.
That wrath might bring them to your city's gate:
Forestall them.

PYRRHUS

No, I'll welcome all with joy
Who in Epirus seek a second Troy.
Let them in muddled hate discern no more

A conquered blood from that which won their war.
Not for the first time will the Greeks, my lord,
Refuse Achilles' deeds their just reward.
Hector once gained by Greek inequity,
And so his son may profit. We shall see.

ORESTES

Then Greece must view you as a rebel son?

PYRRHUS

Am I her lackey, whose battles I have won?

ORESTES

Hermione's eyes, which she will interpose
Between her father and you, will stay your blows.

PYRRHUS

She may be dear to me. But loving her
Does not enslave me to her father, Sir.
I'll hope to find some resolution of
The claims of power and the claims of love.
Sir, visit Helen's daughter; I invite you,
Knowing how closely ties of blood unite you.
That done, my lord, you have my leave to go
And tell the Greeks that my reply is No.

SCENE THREE

PYRRHUS, PHOENIX

PHOENIX

Is it wise that he and his beloved meet?

PYRRHUS

He did, I hear, long worship at her feet.

PHOENIX

What if his love, my lord, were reignited,
And that new-kindled passion were requited?

PYRRHUS

Ah, let them love, dear Phoenix; and let her flee
With him to Sparta, in mutual ecstasy!
Our ports will not detain them. Ah, if she went,
What pain 'twould spare me, what embarrassment!

PHOENIX

My lord—

17

PYRRHUS

We'll soon find time for further speaking;
Andromache's here.

SCENE FOUR

PYRRHUS, ANDROMACHE, CEPHISA

PYRRHUS

> Madam, is it me you're seeking?
> Dare I let such a sweet hope cross my mind?

ANDROMACHE

I'm going to where you keep my son confined.
Since once a day you let me be alone
With all of Hector and of Troy I own,
I was about to weep an hour away
With him. I have not kissed him yet today.

PYRRHUS

Madam, the Greeks are frightened, it appears,
And soon may give you other grounds for tears.

ANDROMACHE

My lord, what fear afflicts them? Tell me, do.
Did some poor Trojan get away from you?

PYRRHUS

Their enmity for Hector is not dead.
They fear his son.

[*Act One · Scene Four*]

ANDROMACHE

A worthy cause for dread!
An infant who does not yet know that he
Is Hector's son, and Pyrrhus' property!

PYRRHUS

The Greeks would have him perish, infant or no,
And Agamemnon's son has told me so.

ANDROMACHE

And will you have that cruel doom proclaimed?
Oh, it's at me, not him, this blow is aimed!
It's not his future vengeance Hellas fears,
But that the boy might dry his mother's tears,
Her sire and husband live in him again:
But all I love must by your hands be slain.

PYRRHUS

Madam, you need not weep. I've sent defiance
To all the Greeks and to their armed alliance;
And should they once again embark, pursuing
Now, with a thousand ships, your son's undoing,
Though it might cost the blood that Helen cost,
A ten years' war, my towers in ashes lost,
I should not hesitate, but should defend
His life against them to my own life's end.
But since, for you, I court such jeopardy,
Can you not look with kindlier eyes on me?
Greece hates me; foes surround me; is it fair
That I've your cruelties as well to bear?
I offer you my sword-arm, hoping too
That you'll accept a heart that worships you.

[*Act One* · *Scene Four*]

Since I am now your champion, tell me, please,
That you are not among my enemies!

ANDROMACHE

What's this, my lord? Should a great heart display
So much of weakness? Think what Greece would say!
Shall your resolve—so noble, so humane—
Appear the impulse of a lovesick brain?
Sad captive that she is, lost in dejection,
How can you wish Andromache's affection?
What charms d'you find in these unhappy eyes,
Which you've condemned to weep until she dies?
No, no: to respect a luckless enemy,
Protect the wretched, restore my child to me,
Against a hundred nations take his part
Without requiring, as your price, my heart,
And, even despite me, guard him with your sword—
Such acts would suit Achilles' son, my lord.

PYRRHUS

What! Has your anger not yet run its course?
Must your hate last forever, and my remorse?
Yes, I have caused some tears; your Phrygian land
Has seen your kindred's blood redden this hand;
But how, beneath your eyes, my heart has bled!
How I have paid for all the tears they've shed!
Under what weight of guilt they've made me bow!
All that I did to Troy I suffer now:
Vanquished, in chains, tormented by regret,
Burning in fires far worse than ever I set,
In tears, in turmoil, in anxiety . . .
When was I ever as cruel as you can be?
But come, enough of trading pains and woes;
Let us unite against our common foes.

Say only, Madam, that I may hope. That done,
I'll free your child, and treat him as my son.
I'll school him to be Troy's avenger! You'll see
Greece punished for its wrongs to you and me.
One glance from you will fire my enterprise:
Your Ilium shall from its cinders rise;
In less time than it took the Greeks to win it,
I'll rebuild Troy, and crown your son within it.

ANDROMACHE

Sir, to such greatness I no more aspire:
'Twas my son's birthright while he had a sire.
O sacred walls my Hector could not save,
Expect no more to see me, now a slave!
With lesser gifts the wretched are content;
What these tears beg, my lord, is banishment—
That far from Greeks, and you, I be exiled
To mourn my husband and to hide my child.
Your love has caused us to be hated, Sir:
Return to Helen's daughter. Marry her.

PYRRHUS

How can I, Madam? Ah, how you rack my soul!
How give her back a heart which you control?
I know my love was promised her; I own
That she came here to share Epirus' throne;
Fate brought you here together, you to be
In slavery's fetters, she to fetter me.
Yet have I given her queenly treatment here?
Would one not rather judge, as things appear,
With you adored, her treated with disdain,
That she's the slave, and that it's you who reign?
Ah, if but one of the sighs I breathe your way
Escaped to her, what joy she would betray!

[*Act One* · *Scene Four*]

ANDROMACHE

Of course she'd welcome sighs from you; why not?
Could all your former service be forgot?
Could slaughtered Trojans make her cold to you,
Or a dead husband to whom her love is due?
And what a husband! What a bitter thought
That by his death your father's fame was bought!
By Hector's blood he lives; you both are known,
Father and son, but by my tears alone.

PYRRHUS

So be it, Madam; I must accommodate you:
I must forget, or, rather, I must hate you.
My passion's grown too fiery, too intense,
Ever to end in mere indifference.
Think well. Unless my heart can from this date
Love with abandon, it must fiercely hate.
In my just rage I'll give more cause to mourn:
The child shall answer for the mother's scorn;
Greece asks for him, and I am in no mood
Forever to protect ingratitude.

ANDROMACHE

Alas, then he must die! His sole defense
Lies in his mother's tears, his innocence;
Perhaps his death, so weary have I grown,
Will end my miseries and bring my own.
For him I have prolonged my life, my pain;
Now, in his steps, I'll seek his sire again.
We three, my lord, shall once again be one,
Through your kind offices—

PYRRHUS

                Madam, go see your son.
Concern for him may make your heart decide
No more to let resentment be its guide.
I shall return to hear our fates declared:
Think, as you hold him, how he might be spared.

SCENE ONE

HERMIONE, CLEONE

HERMIONE

Since you insist, I'll see him. I agree
Once more to grant him that felicity.
Pylades soon will show him to this place;
And yet my impulse is to shun his face.

CLEONE

How could the sight of him cause you any ill?
Is he not, Madam, the same Orestes still
Whose coming you've desired, whose constant love
You've often missed and spoken sadly of?

HERMIONE

That love, which I so coldly cast aside,
Renders this visit painful to my pride.
What shame I'll suffer; how he'll gloat to see
My sad plight match his former misery!
"Is this the proud Hermione?," he'll cry.
"She scorned me once; now she's as scorned as I.
She who so haughtily withheld her heart
Learns in her turn how such disdain can smart!"
O gods!

CLEONE

Ah, Madam, dismiss that needless fear.
What! Would a suitor come to mock and jeer?
Your beauty's power still holds him in its sway.
The heart he brings, he could not take away.
But tell me what your father's message said.

HERMIONE

If Pyrrhus still puts off the day we'll wed,
And will not let the Trojan brat be slain,
The Greeks, I'm told, must take me home again.

CLEONE

Then, Madam, hear Orestes, who's your friend.
What Pyrrhus started, you at least can end.
A breach is certain; therefore anticipate him.
Have you not told me that you've come to hate him?

HERMIONE

Hate him, Cleone? In honor, how could I not?
After so many favors, all forgot,
He whom I've held so dear breaks every vow!
I've loved him too much not to hate him now.

CLEONE

Then flee him, Madam; Orestes loves you yet—

HERMIONE

Ah, give my anger time to strengthen! Let
Me stiffen my resolve against my foe;

I want to loathe him by the time I go.
The wretch will give me cause; 'twill not take long.

CLEONE

What! Are you waiting, then, for some new wrong?
He loves a captive, and he flaunts it, too;
Does that not make him odious to you?
How can he worse offend you? If you *could*
Detest the traitor, you already would.

HERMIONE

Ah, cruel creature, why rack my anguished thought?
My own mind frightens me, it's so distraught.
Try not to credit what you see in me;
Believe my love is dead, that I am free,
That I have steeled my heart against the man;
Make me believe it also, if you can.
You'd have me flee. Let's go, then! What detains me?
His conquest of a slave no longer pains me;
And may that slave enchain him with her beauty;
Come then . . . But if the wretch recalled his duty!
If he recovered his fidelity!
If he should sue for pardon at my knee!
If, Eros, thou couldst bind him to obey me!
If . . . No, the ingrate lives but to betray me.
Well then, to mar their happiness, let us stay;
Let's find some joy by standing in their way;
Or, forcing him to break his solemn pledge,
Let's make all Greece condemn his sacrilege.
Already I've drawn their wrath upon the son;
They shall demand the mother, before I'm done;
She'll pay for all I've suffered, eye for eye;
May she destroy him, or through his folly die.

[*Act Two* · *Scene One*]

CLEONE

D'you think her eyes, which weep each day and hour,
Rejoice in challenging your beauty's power,
Or that a heart on which such sorrow lies
Solicited her persecutor's sighs?
D'you think his sighs afford her heart relief?
Why is she then so overwhelmed by grief?
If he attracts her, why does she treat him coldly?

HERMIONE

Alas, I put my trust in all he told me.
I played no reticent and cautious part:
I thought that I could safely bare my heart,
And so, without a moment's feigned austerity,
I told him what I felt in plain sincerity.
And who would not have done so, once she'd heard
His love declared upon his sacred word?
Ah, did he see me then as now he does?
Recall how all conspired to plead his cause:
My family avenged, Greece wild with joy,
Our ships all laden with the spoils of Troy,
His father's glorious deeds by his outshone,
His love, which seemed more ardent than my own,
And you, my heart, so dazzled by his fame—
All these deceived me, ere he did the same.
Ah well, Cleone, whatever Pyrrhus be,
Orestes' virtues touch Hermione.
He staunchly loves me, though without return;
To love him back is something I may learn.
So, let him come.

CLEONE

Why, Madam, he is here.

30

HERMIONE

Ah! I had not supposed he was so near.

SCENE TWO

HERMIONE, ORESTES, CLEONE

HERMIONE

May a sad princess fancy that some trace
Of former love has brought you to this place?
Or is it duty alone that I should see
In your most welcome haste to visit me?

ORESTES

What brings me is my blind, love-stricken soul;
You know, my lady, that it's my destined role
Always to seek you out, whom I adore,
And ever vow to seek you out no more.
I know your glance will cause old wounds to flow;
Each step toward you is perjury, I know;
I blush for it; and yet those gods could tell
Who saw the frenzy of my last farewell,
That I have sped wherever certain doom
Might keep my vows for me and end my gloom.
I've begged for death where cruel tribes appease
With human blood their brutal deities:
They barred me from their altars, and would not spend
The blood I should have been content to lend.
At last I've come to seek within your eyes
The death I chase, and which forever flies.
Let them look coldly, and my prize is won:
If they deny me hope, the deed is done;

32

If they would end my quest, and see me dead,
They need but say what they have always said.
You see what urge has driven me all this year.
Madam, your victim stands before you here.
The Scythians might have cheated you of me
Had they not lacked your heartless cruelty.

HERMIONE

Come, no more dismal talk, my lord. Greece sent
You here to deal with things more exigent.
Enough of Scythia, and my heartlessness!
Think of the kings whose will you must express.
Is their revenge less pressing than your pique?
D'you think that it's Orestes' blood they seek?
Discharge the duties of your embassy.

ORESTES

Pyrrhus discharges my demands and me,
Madam. He sends me home. Some power has won
Him over to the cause of Hector's son.

HERMIONE

The traitor!

ORESTES

Thus I've come to you to find,
Before I go, what fate I am assigned.
Even before you speak, I think that I
Can hear the cold disdain of your reply.

HERMIONE

Must your sad speeches evermore complain
Unjustly of my spite and my disdain?

Where is this coldness which you so resent?
Epirus was to me a banishment;
My father sent me hither; how do you know
That I've not since, in secret, shared your woe?
D'you think that you alone have grieved, that I
Have not found reason, here, to mourn and sigh?
Who tells you that I have not wished, despite
My duty, that your ship would heave in sight?

ORESTES

You've wished to see me! Ah, Princess, can this be?
How can such welcome words be meant for me?
Orestes stands before you! Open your eyes!
Behold Orestes, whom you so despise.

HERMIONE

Yes, it is you, whose passion first revealed
To me what power these eyes of mine might wield;
You whose great virtues I was conscious of;
You whom I've pitied, whom I could wish to love.

ORESTES

I well see what's to be my sorry part:
I have your wishes, Pyrrhus has your heart.

HERMIONE

Ah, do not wish that you were Pyrrhus, for
I'd hate you then.

ORESTES

                    And love me all the more.
With what changed eyes you'd view my qualities!

34

You wish to love me, and I cannot please;
Ah, but if Love were master of your will,
Though you might wish to hate, you'd love me still.
Gods! What devotion, tender and sincere,
Might plead for me if you could only hear!
What argues now for Pyrrhus? Only you,
Despite yourself, no doubt despite him too:
For now he hates you; another suits his whim . . .

HERMIONE

Who says, my lord, that I am scorned by him?
Has he by look or word declared as much?
D'you think my charms contemptible, and such
As cannot long inspire a heart to love me?
Others, perhaps, may judge more highly of me.

ORESTES

Go on, insult my love. That's nobly done.
Is it my heart that scorns you, cruel one?
Have not your eyes beheld my faithfulness?
Does my enslavement prove them powerless?
When have I scorned them? Ah, how they would shine
If but my rival felt such scorn as mine!

HERMIONE

What care I for his love or hate, my lord?
Go. Give his rebel pride its just reward;
Arm all of Greece against him, and destroy
Epirus. Make of it a second Troy.
Will you say I love him, now that I've spoken so?

35

ORESTES

Do more than speak, my lady; you too must go.
Why linger as a hostage on this shore?
Come, let your eyes inflame the Greeks to war,
And let one hatred join us—you and me.

HERMIONE

But if he, meanwhile, weds Andromache?

ORESTES

What, Madam?

HERMIONE

Only think of our disgrace,
Should he espouse a Phrygian in my place!

ORESTES

Hah! And you claim to hate him! Madam, speak true:
Love is a fire the heart can't hide from view:
Words, silence, looks, all give away the game,
And fires, half smothered, burst into brighter flame.

HERMIONE

My lord, how doggedly you misconstrue
My words, and make them poisonous to you,
Detecting hidden twists in all I state,
And finding love concealed beneath my hate.
Well, here's plain truth, on which I bid you act.
My duty brought me here; you'll grant that fact.
Duty detains me. I cannot leave this land
Till Pyrrhus, or my sire, shall so command.

36

Go tell the king that Father will not marry
A child of his to Greece's adversary;
Force him to choose the Trojan boy, or me.
He cannot keep us both; which shall it be?
Let him yield the boy to you, or send me hence.
Farewell. I'll follow you, if he consents.

SCENE THREE

Yes, yes, you'll follow me; the king will give
His prompt consent; of that I'm positive.
Pyrrhus will not detain her, never fear:
He has no eyes but for his Trojan dear.
All other women weary him; he'll snatch
At any chance to annul the wedding match.
I need but broach the matter. And then, what bliss
To rob Epirus of a prize like this!
Keep all that's left of Hector's Troy; protect
Sons, widows by the thousand; I shan't object,
Epirus, if Hermione can but sever
Her fortunes from your lord, and you, forever.
But here, by chance, he comes. I'll speak with him.
To all her charms, Love, let his eyes be dim.

SCENE FOUR

PYRRHUS

Ah, there you are, my lord. I must avow
That I dismissed your arguments just now
Too brusquely; since we spoke, I've come to see
That all your words had truth and cogency;
That, as you said, I was an infidel
To Greece, Achilles, and myself as well,
And might undo, by fostering Troy once more,
All that my sire and I had battled for.
No longer shall I flout the Greeks' just ire.
You'll have, my lord, the victim you desire.

ORESTES

With that wise, stern resolve, my lord, you buy
A peace for which a luckless child must die.

PYRRHUS

Yes, and I wish still firmer ties to Greece:
Hermione is the pledge of lasting peace,
And I shall wed her. How fitting, Sir, to plight
Our troth with you as witness to the rite.
You'll represent the Greeks; her father, too,
Who sees his brother live again in you.

Go, and prepare her for tomorrow, Sir,
When, with your blessing, I'll wed both Greece and her.

ORESTES

O gods!

SCENE FIVE

PYRRHUS

Well, Phoenix, does Love now tyrannize me?
And are you able now to recognize me?

PHOENIX

I am. By righteous wrath you've been restored
Both to the Greeks and to yourself, my lord.
I see no helpless toy of passion here,
But the great Pyrrhus, Achilles' son and peer,
Who, grown once more commanding and sublime,
Now triumphs over Troy a second time.

PYRRHUS

Say, rather, that my triumphs now begin.
It's this day's work alone I glory in;
My proud heart, once enslaved, now overthrows
A love more dangerous than a thousand foes.
Think, Phoenix, from what troubles I am freed,
What a great host of evils Love can breed,
What ties, what friendships I was about to break,
What risks I blindly courted for her sake!
All Greece was leagued against one rebel, and I
Was eager, for the love of her, to die.

41

PHOENIX

I bless, my lord, her timely cruelty;
It has preserved you—

PYRRHUS

      Look how she's dealt with me.
I thought that, after an hour with her child,
Her anxious mother-love would make her mild.
I went to see her. Was I better treated?
It was with tears and rage that I was greeted.
Wilder and bitterer her woe became;
A hundred times she uttered Hector's name.
I swore I'd save her son, but all in vain:
"Hector," she'd cry, and clutch the boy again.
"Behold his eyes, his mouth, his brave young face;
'Tis he, 'tis you, dear husband, I embrace."
What does she think? That I'll be guardian of
A son who keeps alive her wifely love?

PHOENIX

That's her ungrateful plan, it would appear.
But, Sir, forget her.

PYRRHUS

      What gives her hope is clear:
She counts upon her beauty to appease
My wrath, and bring me back upon my knees.
Phoenix, she'd kneel to *me* in vain; I've done
With Hector's widow; I am Achilles' son.
There's too much hate dividing her and me.

PHOENIX

Good. Speak no more, then, of Andromache.
Go to Hermione, give her joy at last,
And at her feet forget the angry past.
You should yourself prepare her to be wed,
Rather than send a rival in your stead
Who loves her dearly.

PYRRHUS

                              Would my marriage make
Andromache feel jealous for my sake?

PHOENIX

What! Is Andromache always on your brain?
Why be concerned about her joy or pain?
What spell compels your thoughts to turn her way?

PYRRHUS

No, I've not said to her all that I must say.
She has but glimpsed my wrath; nor does she know
How utterly I have become her foe.
Let us go back. I'll face her, and in straight,
Harsh terms express the fullness of my hate.
Come, see her beauty spurned and put to rout,
Dear Phoenix.

PHOENIX

                              Go, my lord; I have no doubt
You'll kneel before her, swear your love again,
And give her fresh occasion for disdain.

43

PYRRHUS

I see; you think, then, that my heart pursues her
Just as before, and gladly would excuse her.

PHOENIX

My lord, you love her.

PYRRHUS

                    That thankless woman? No!
My every kindness makes her hatred grow.
No kin, no friends protect her, only I;
I could—nay, should—condemn her son to die;
She's but an alien here, a wretched thrall;
I offer her my heart, her son, my all,
And yet am cast by her ungrateful soul
Forever in the persecutor's role.
No, no, my vengeful wrath shall not abate;
I mean, for once, to justify her hate.
I'll give the Greeks her son. What tears will rain
At that! What names she'll call me, in her pain!
'Twill be the best of all her tragic scenes . . .
Phoenix, 'twill kill her; and I shall be the means
Whereby a knife is plunged into her heart.

PHOENIX

Sir, if you lack the will to play your part,
Why make so brash a statement of intent?

PYRRHUS

Quite so. Forgive that twinge of sentiment.
Were you afraid it might deflect my ire?
'Twas the last flicker of a dying fire.

44

Come, Phoenix, I'll obey you. Counsel me.
Must I yield the boy? And wed Hermione?

PHOENIX

Yes, yes, my lord, go see her; tell her that you
Most humbly—

PYRRHUS

All that I've promised, I shall do.

SCENE ONE

PYLADES

My lord, restrain this fury. Let me advise you.
You're not yourself; I hardly recognize you.
Do hear me.

ORESTES

　　　No, wise counsel's out of season.
I'm sick to death of listening to reason.
Too long my life's dragged on in pain, and my
Resolve is to abduct her, or to die.
My mind's made up; I'll do it, Pylades,
I'll do it.

PYLADES

　　　Well, we'll abduct her, then; but please
Remember meanwhile where you are, and how
You'd seem to anyone who saw you now.
Put down your feelings; don't be overwrought;
Forbid your eyes to give away your thought.
These guards, this court, this very atmosphere
Report to Pyrrhus, and you must also fear
Hermione; conceal your rage from her.
Why were you seeking her, frenzied as you were?

49

ORESTES

Who knows? Half-mad, I had no clear intent.
In my exasperation, perhaps I meant
To utter threats against her and the king.

PYLADES

Would that, Sir, have accomplished anything?

ORESTES

No, no, but tell me: whose wits would not be strained
By such a blow as I have just sustained?
Tomorrow, he says, he'll wed Hermione;
He wishes to receive her hand from me!
Oh, sooner will my hand, my bloody sword—

PYLADES

You blame him for this twist of fate, my lord;
But he, who hates what prudence makes him do,
May well deserve one's pity as much as you.

ORESTES

No, no, to spite me is his aim and spur:
He'd scorn her were I not in love with her;
Till now, he's been oblivious to her charms:
He weds her now to tear her from my arms.
O gods! I'd all but won her, and she might
Have fled with me forever from his sight;
Her heart, so torn 'twixt love and enmity,
Had he rebuffed her, would have turned to me;
Her eyes were opening, Pylades; her breast
Was moved to pity. A word had done the rest.

PYLADES

You think so?

ORESTES

       Think so! Ah, with what rage she swore
To make that traitor—

PYLADES

        She never loved him more.
Had Pyrrhus let you take her, don't you know
That she'd have found some pretext not to go?
Heed me, and shun her wiles; forget your plan
To bear her off; escape her while you can.
Why, Sir, be saddled with a fury who
Will loathe you bitterly, your whole life through,
Remembering the king she almost wed?

ORESTES

That's why I must abduct her, as I said.
All things would smile upon her, did I not,
While fruitless rage would once more be my lot,
And seeking to forget her, all in vain.
No, she must be the partner of my pain.
Enough of pity; enough of lonely sighs;
She in her turn must fear me, and her eyes,
Her cruel eyes, which henceforth I condemn
To tears, shall curse me as I've cursed at them.

PYLADES

So this is how your mission is to end:
Orestes the abductor!

ORESTES

Why not, my friend?
If Greece, avenged, gave thanks for my success,
That thankless woman would wring my heart no less;
And what to me were Hellas' high acclaim,
If all Epirus were to mock my name?
What choice have I? But, to speak openly,
My innocence begins to weary me.
Why, always, must an unjust providence
Let evil be and punish innocence?
When I review my life, I everywhere
Find woes and pains which prove the gods unfair.
Well, now I'll give them something to resent;
Let crime's rewards precede its punishment!
But you, friend, why call down upon your head
The lightnings that are meant for me instead?
Too much, too long, my friendship's burdened you:
Avoid my doomed and guilty person, do.
Pity, dear Pylades, must not blind your eyes.
Mine be these perils, since I shall claim the prize.
Convey this child the king has yielded me
To Greece.

PYLADES

Come, let's abduct Hermione.
Courage, my lord, wins every perilous test.
What cannot friendship do at love's behest?
Go brace your Greeks for action; bid them prepare.
Our ships are ready, and the wind stands fair.
I know this palace, its mazelike rooms and halls:
The sea comes beating to its very walls;
Tonight, with ease, I shall conduct your prey
Aboard your vessel by a secret way.

ORESTES

Friend, I abuse your friendship. Forgive my great
Troubles, which you alone compassionate;
Pardon a wretch who harms what he adores,
Whom all men hate, whom he himself abhors.
Some happier day, I hope I may reward—

PYLADES

Conceal your thoughts; that's all I ask, my lord.
Don't let your plan be guessed before we start.
Till then, forget Hermione's thankless heart.
Forget your love. Ah, look; she's coming, Sir.

ORESTES

Go, then. I'll see to myself. You see to her.

SCENE TWO

HERMIONE, ORESTES, CLEONE

ORESTES

Well, Madam, the king is yours again; I've met
With Pyrrhus, and your wedding hour is set.

HERMIONE

So I've been told; and I have also heard
That you were seeking me to bring this word.

ORESTES

You're not averse to marrying him now?

HERMIONE

Whoever dreamt that he would keep his vow?
That, thus belatedly, his love would show?
That he would claim me, just when I planned to go?
I think, as you do, that he fears the Greeks,
That it's his interest, not his heart, that speaks,
And that your love for me was ever stronger.

ORESTES

No, Madam, he loves you. I question that no longer.
What heart is proof against your charms? And your
Intent's not been to displease him, I am sure.

54

HERMIONE

What can I do? My hand's been promised, Sir:
Can I take back what I did not confer?
A princess' heart may not decide her fate:
Her only glory is to obey the state.
Yet, for your sake, I all but fled; you saw
How close I came to breaking duty's law.

ORESTES

Ah, cruel one, you knew that . . . Madam, you know
Our hearts are in our power to bestow.
Your heart was yours. I hoped; and yet I see
That this your choice entails no slight to me.
Therefore I blame not you but providence,
And shall not weary you with my laments.
You rightly do your duty; mine I'll do
By sparing you a mournful interview.

SCENE THREE

HERMIONE, CLEONE

HERMIONE

Had you supposed he'd be so self-possessed?

CLEONE

Grief is most dangerous when it's unexpressed.
I pity him the more, since through his own
Kind agency his hopes were overthrown.
Think for how long your nuptials were delayed!
Orestes spoke then, and the king was swayed.

HERMIONE

You think that fear has swayed him. What is it he fears?
Nations who fled from Hector ten long years?
Who, when Achilles was not by their side,
Took to their burning vessels, terrified,
And who would, but for Pyrrhus, still be seen
Asking at Troy for Menelaus' queen?
No, he fears nothing. All that he does is of
His own free will; if he weds, he weds for love.
Let glum Orestes blame me for his grief:
From that sad subject is there no relief?
Dearest Cleone, Pyrrhus returns to us!
Conceive how glad I am, how rapturous!
Think what a man our Pyrrhus is! Recall

56

His many exploits . . . Who could count them all?
Intrepid, crowned by victory everywhere,
Charming, and faithful, he is beyond compare.
Think—

CLEONE

Hide your feelings, for your rival nears,
Meaning, no doubt, to bathe your feet with tears.

HERMIONE

Gods! May I not give vent to my delight?
Let's leave: what could I say to her?

SCENE FOUR

ANDROMACHE, HERMIONE, CLEONE, CEPHISA

ANDROMACHE

                                        Why take flight,
My lady? Will it not gladden you to see
Great Hector's widow weeping at your knee?
I do not come with jealous, tearful eyes
To envy you the heart that's now your prize.
I saw, alas, Achilles' cruel sword
Transfix the only heart that mine adored:
Hector it was who set my heart on fire,
And in his tomb I've buried my desire.
Yet I still have a son. Someday you'll know,
Madam, how strong a mother's love can grow;
But you shall not, I hope, have cause to learn
What dread she feels, what anguishing concern,
When every comfort's lost to her, save one,
And men conspire to rob her of her son.
Hear me: when, sick of ten years' bloody strife,
The angry Trojans sought your mother's life,
I bade my Hector come to her defense:
You could, with Pyrrhus, wield such influence.
Why do they fear a babe who's fatherless?
Oh, let me hide him in some wilderness,
Some desert isle; they may be sure that I
Will teach him nothing but to weep and sigh.

HERMIONE

I feel for you; but duty curbs my will,
And when my father has spoken, I must be still.
It's he who's prompted Pyrrhus' wrath. But who
Could touch the heart of Pyrrhus as well as you?
His soul has long been subject to your spell.
Persuade him, Madam, and I'll concur. Farewell.

SCENE FIVE

ANDROMACHE, CEPHISA

ANDROMACHE

How coldly she refused to hear my cries!

CEPHISA

Take her advice; find Pyrrhus, and let your eyes
With one look rout both her and Greece. But see,
He comes to *you*.

SCENE SIX

PYRRHUS, ANDROMACHE, PHOENIX, CEPHISA

PYRRHUS *(to Phoenix)*

Well, where's Hermione?
Did you not say she'd be here at this hour?

PHOENIX

So I believed.

ANDROMACHE *(to Cephisa)*

Behold my eyes' great power!

PYRRHUS *(to Phoenix)*

What did she say?

ANDROMACHE

Alas! All hope is gone!

PHOENIX

Sire, we must find the princess. Let's move on.

[*Act Three · Scene Six*]

CEPHISA

Why be so stubborn? Speak.

ANDROMACHE

                   He's sworn to let
Them take my son.

CEPHISA

That hasn't happened yet.

ANDROMACHE

No, no, his death's decreed; my tears are vain.

PYRRHUS *(to Phoenix)*

She will not even look at us. What disdain!

ANDROMACHE

I but increase his rage; let's go in peace.

PYRRHUS *(to Phoenix)*

Come, let us yield up Hector's son to Greece.

ANDROMACHE

Ah, wait, my lord! What can you mean to do?
If you yield the son, why not the mother too?
You lately pledged me friendship, vow on vow;
Can you not spare so much as pity, now?
Am I condemned? May no appeal be heard?

PYRRHUS

Phoenix will tell you that I've given my word.

ANDROMACHE

How many perils you said you'd face for me!

PYRRHUS

Then I was blind; but now my eyes can see.
For you, I would have spared the boy this fate,
But you'd not deign to ask me. It's too late.

ANDROMACHE

Sir, well you understood the sighs I sighed,
The tears I wept lest hope should be denied.
Forgive me if my former lofty state
Left me too proud to beg and supplicate.
You know that, but for you, Andromache
Would never have embraced a master's knee.

PYRRHUS

No, 'twas not pride but hate; you could not owe
A debt to one whom you detested so.
This very son you cherish and caress—
If I had saved him, you would love him less.
On all sides now I'm hated, scorned, maligned:
You hate me more than all the Greeks combined.
I leave you to your fury. Enjoy it, pray.
Come, Phoenix.

ANDROMACHE

Let us rejoin my husband.

CEPHISA

Stay,
My lady . . .

ANDROMACHE

What could I say but what he knows,
Who is the only author of my woes?
(To Pyrrhus)
Behold, Sir, how through you I am abased.
I've seen my father dead, our walls laid waste,
My kinsmen perish through your battle lust,
My husband's bleeding corpse dragged in the dust.
Now only one small slave, his son, remains.
For him I chose to live, although in chains,
And was at times consoled to think that fate
Had exiled me in no more barbarous state;
That, blest in his mischance, my son might find,
Though captive here, a master just and kind,
Who would not be his jailor but his shield.
To Priam's pleas Achilles deigned to yield:
How kind, I thought, Achilles' son must be . . .
Forgive, dear Hector, my credulity!
I had not dreamt your foe could wrong me thus;
In spite of all, I thought him generous.
Ah, if he only would permit us to
Expire beside the tomb I've raised to you,
And, ending thus his hatred and our pain,
Let us in faithful dust be one again!

PYRRHUS

Go, Phoenix; I'll follow.

SCENE SEVEN

PYRRHUS *(continuing)*
                Stay, Madam, if you will.
The son you weep for can be salvaged still.
I fear that, when I caused your tears to start,
I only gave you arms against my heart,
Which I had thought secure in enmity.
But do, my lady, turn your eyes on me.
Tell me, is this the face of a stern judge,
Or of a foe who bears a bitter grudge?
Why force me to afflict you? Let us make
An end of hatred, for your son's poor sake.
Preserve him, Madam; it's I who urge you to.
Must I with sighs request his life of you?
Must I embrace your knees, beseech and moan?
For the last time, save his life and save your own.
I know what pledges I shall violate,
That for your sake I'll face a storm of hate.
I'll send Hermione back, conferring òn her
No queenly crown, but insult and dishonor,
And in the temple where she was to wed
I'll set her bridal chaplet on your head.
But, Madam, what I offer you'll disdain
No longer: you must choose to die or reign.
After a year's ingratitude, I'll not
Put up with further doubts as to my lot.
Enough of hopes, fears, threats, and wasted breath.

Your loss would kill me; yet to wait is death.
Think well, my lady: I'll come when you have done
And lead you to the temple, with your son,
Where, as your groom or in a fiercer guise,
I'll crown you, or have him slain before your eyes.

SCENE EIGHT

ANDROMACHE, CEPHISA

CEPHISA

I told you that, despite the Greeks, you'd be
Once more the mistress of your destiny.

ANDROMACHE

Alas! You see where your advice has led!
Now, through my fault, my child's blood shall be shed.

CEPHISA

Madam, your faithfulness persists too long:
Excess of any virtue can be wrong.
Hector himself would urge you to comply.

ANDROMACHE

And marry Pyrrhus in his place? Not I!

CEPHISA

Not for your son, whose life's in jeopardy?
D'you think that Hector's shade would blush to see
You wed a conquering king who will restore
The sceptered rank which once your family bore,
Who'll tread your Grecian foes into the mire,

Forget that fierce Achilles was his sire,
Disown his deeds, and bid them be forgot?

ANDROMACHE

He may forget those deeds, but I cannot.
Hector's dishonored corpse—how not recall
Who dragged it round and round our city wall?
How not remember Priam fallen dead
Across his altar, staining it with red?
Think, think, Cephisa, of that night which for
A slaughtered nation ended nevermore;
Imagine Pyrrhus, his eyes aglint with flame
As through our burning palaces he came,
Over my brothers' bodies picked his way
And, drenched with blood, still urged his men to slay;
Hear too the victors' shouts, their victims' cries
Cut short by flame or sword; and let your eyes
Find, in that hell, half-crazed Andromache:
That was how Pyrrhus first appeared to me;
Such were the deeds for which Fame wreathed his brow;
Such is the man you'd have me marry now.
No, I'll not share his bloodguilt. Let him kill
Us, as his final victims, if that's his will.
I can't blot out such horrors and be his wife.

CEPHISA

Come then, and see your dear son lose his life.
They bide your answer . . . Madam, what makes you start?

ANDROMACHE

You've waked a memory that stops my heart.
Cephisa! Can I watch them kill my boy,
Dear Hector's image and my only joy?

68

His son, the pledge of our fidelity?
Ah, I recall how on the day when he
Strode forth to meet Achilles and to die,
He held his son, and kissed the babe good-bye:
"Dear wife," he said, wiping my tears away,
"I know not what my fate shall be today;
This son, this pledge of love, I leave behind me:
If I am lost to him, through you he'll find me.
Tell him how in our days of happiness
You loved his father; and love my son no less."
How can I see this precious life undone,
And all Troy's lineage perish with my son?
O barbarous king, why must he bear my guilt?
Because I hate you, must his blood be spilt?
Has he bewailed the kin you would not spare?
Taxed you with crimes of which he's unaware?
But oh, my son, you die unless the blade
He holds above your head is somehow stayed.
I could avert it; and can I see you slain?
No, you'll not die; I could not bear that pain.
Let's go find Pyrrhus. But no: Cephisa, pray
Go find him for me.

CEPHISA

What would you have me say?

ANDROMACHE

Tell him I love my son so much that I . . .
D'you think he means it, that my son must die?
Could passion make a man so barbarous?

CEPHISA

Madam, he'll soon come raging back to us.

69

ANDROMACHE

Go then, and say—

CEPHISA

Say what? That you'll wed the king?

ANDROMACHE

Alas! Am I free to promise such a thing?
O ashes of my husband! O Father! O Troy!
Ah, but your life could cost me dear, my boy.
Come.

CEPHISA

Where, my lady? What have you decided?

ANDROMACHE

I'll kneel at Hector's tomb, and there be guided.

SCENE ONE

ANDROMACHE, CEPHISA

CEPHISA

No doubt of it, Madam; it's your husband who
Has brought about this miracle in you.
It's Hector's will that Troy should from its grave
Rise, through the blessèd son he bids you save.
Pyrrhus has sworn to give him back; you heard
Him swear it. He waited only for your word.
Trust in his passion: his father's deeds, his crown,
His allies—at your feet he lays them down;
He makes you ruler of his heart and state.
Does such a conqueror deserve your hate?
Already, braving all the Greeks, he's shown
That he'll protect your dear son as his own;
Risking his own security, he has bade
His royal bodyguard to shield the lad.
But come now; at the temple, everyone
Awaits you.

ANDROMACHE

I'll go; but first I'll see my son.

CEPHISA

My lady, where's the hurry? Henceforth you'll see
Your son whenever you wish; you shall be free

73

To give him countless kisses, and express
At leisure all a mother's tenderness.
What joy to have a child whom you may raise
Not as a slave who cringes and obeys,
But as a prince whose kingly blood will tell!

ANDROMACHE

Come. I must bid my son a last farewell.

CEPHISA

O gods! What are you saying?

ANDROMACHE

     Cephisa dear,
I keep no secrets from your loyal ear.
You've been a faithful friend in all my woes,
But I thought you knew me better. Did you suppose
That the dear husband who thought to live in me
Could be betrayed by his Andromache;
That I could cause the dead of Troy to weep
And could, to ease my lot, disturb their sleep?
Was it such love I vowed to Hector's shade?
But, doomed to die, his son required my aid,
And I, by marrying Pyrrhus, shall secure
A sworn protector for him; of that I'm sure.
I know the king, Cephisa. Fierce, but sincere,
He'll more than keep his bargain, never fear.
I count too on the Greeks: their hate and ire
Ensure to Hector's child a second sire.
Since, then, I must be sacrificed, I'll give
To Pyrrhus, for so long as I shall live,
My troth; and he, in pledging his, shall make
My son his own, by bonds that cannot break.
And then this hand shall, harming none but me,

74

Cut short my life, my infidelity;
I'll save my virtue, and to husband, son,
Pyrrhus, myself, my duty shall be done.
There is the innocent stratagem I've planned:
There's what I heard my husband's shade command.
I shall rejoin him and our kings of old.
Cephisa, close my eyes when I am cold.

CEPHISA

Ah, Madam, do not ask that I live on—

ANDROMACHE

No, no, you're not to follow me; when I'm gone,
My only treasure will be in your care.
You've lived for me; live on for Hector's heir.
In him, you'll guard the hopes of Troy; reflect
How long a line of kings you must protect!
Stand watch on Pyrrhus; make him keep his trust:
If need be, speak of me, and say that he must
Respect the troth which by his wish we plighted;
Say that before I died we were united;
That he must not be bitter; that I've done
Much honor to him by leaving him my son.
Inform my son of forebears who were great,
And whom he should be moved to emulate:
Tell him what exploits brought them fame, and bid
Him prize not what they were but what they did;
Speak daily of his father's virtues; tell
Him something, now and then, of me as well.
But let him dream no vengeance for our race:
He'll have a master, and must mind his place,
Nor be too boastful of the Trojan past.
He is of Hector's lineage, but the last—
The last of Ilium, for the sake whereof
I've sacrificed my life, my hate, my love.

75

[*Act Four* · *Scene One*]

CEPHISA, *crying*

Ahh!

ANDROMACHE

Do not attend me, if your heart foresees
That it could not hold back such tears as these.
Someone is coming. Cephisa, cease your weeping.
Remember that my secret's in your keeping.
Ah, it's Hermione. Let us flee her spite.

SCENE TWO

CLEONE

Your silence, Madam, astonishes me quite.
You still say nothing. Can the brutal scorn
Which he has shown you be so calmly borne?
How can you brook this, you who used to be
Chilled by the mention of Andromache;
You who were in despair if you heard say
That Pyrrhus had so much as glanced her way?
He weds her now, and crowns her—gives her, too,
Vows which an hour ago belonged to you,
And yet you seal your lips and will not deign,
Despite the blow you've suffered, to complain!
It frightens me when angry lips are dumb.
Oh, how much better—

HERMIONE

       Have you bid Orestes come?

CLEONE

He's coming, Madam, he's coming—and he'll be your
Devoted slave as ever, you may be sure,
Eager to serve you without hope or fee:
Your eyes still hold him in captivity.
But here he is.

SCENE THREE

ORESTES

Ah, Madam, is it true
That by your wish, for once, I visit you?
Or did a flattering hope deceive my ear?
Do you indeed desire my presence here?
Can I believe that eyes which once abhorred
The sight of me—

HERMIONE

Do you love me still, my lord?

ORESTES

Do I love you? Gods! The oaths I swore in vain,
My flight and my return to you, my pain,
The tearful tribute that my eyes have paid you—
What proofs do you need, if these do not persuade you?

HERMIONE

Avenge me, and I'll believe them all.

ORESTES

> Then for
> Your cause let's go and rouse all Greece once more,
> And let us by my deeds and your acclaim
> Match Helen's glory and Agamemnon's fame.
> We'll make this land, like Troy, weep scalding tears,
> And prove ourselves to be our fathers' peers.
> Come then, I'm ready.

HERMIONE

> No, my lord, we'll stay.
> Insulted thus, I shall not slink away.
> What! Shall I flee my insolent foes, and go
> Elsewhere to seek a vengeance far too slow?
> Shall I invest my hopes of vengeance in
> A war which, after all, we might not win?
> If you'd avenge me, do it now. I'll leave
> Only when all this land has cause to grieve.
> Come, to delay is to refuse me. Fly
> To the temple. You must kill—

ORESTES

> Whom?

HERMIONE

> Pyrrhus.

ORESTES

> I
> Kill Pyrrhus, Madam?

HERMIONE

Is your resolve so slack?
Go, go; be quick, lest I should call you back.
Don't speak to me of sacred rights and laws;
It's surely not for you to plead his cause.

ORESTES

How could I plead for him, Madam, when your kind
Favors have etched his crimes upon my mind?
Let's be avenged, but not as you propose;
Let us be not his murderers but his foes,
And justly punish him by means of war.
What! Shall I, as the Greeks' ambassador,
Take them, for answer, Pyrrhus' severed head?
Was it my mission to strike a monarch dead?
No, no, let Greece denounce him, and let him be
Crushed by a people's righteous enmity.
Kings, Madam, who by the will of Heaven reign—

HERMIONE

Is it not enough, Sir, that I wish him slain?
That I insist on having, to atone
For my smirched honor, a victim all my own?
That for this tyrant's death I'll give my hand?
That I detest him?—which means, you understand,
That once I loved him. The scoundrel won me, whether
By my heart's wish, or Father's, or both together,
It does not matter. But heed what I have said.
Although my faith's been shamefully misled,
Though I abhor his crime, while he shall live,
Beware, Sir, lest I weaken and forgive.
Till he is dead, mistrust my heart. I may
Love him tomorrow, unless he dies today.

ORESTES

Why then, lest you forgive him, he must die;
I must . . . But how to do it? How shall I
On such short notice serve your angry whim?
How shall my sword-blade hew a path to him?
I've just arrived here, and at once I learn
That there's an empire I must overturn,
That I must slay a king, and that in one
Short day, one hour, one moment, it must be done;
That I must cut him down in public view!
Well, let me first escort my victim to
The altar. Later, I'll do your will. I need
To reconnoiter, and to plan the deed.
Tonight, tonight, I'll slay him; you shall see.

HERMIONE

Meanwhile, today, he weds Andromache;
Already, in the temple, they've raised his throne,
My shame is published, and his crime is known.
Why wait then, Sir? He offers you his head:
He goes unarmed, unguarded, to be wed;
Round Hector's son his men are all arrayed;
He risks the stroke of any vengeful blade.
Why be more careful of his life than he?
Go, arm your Greeks, and those I brought with me;
Stir up your friends; all mine are at your call.
He wrongs me, mocks you, and insults us all.
Our partisans already share my hate,
And will not spare a Trojan woman's mate.
They'll bring your foe to bay, or if you like
You've but to turn them loose and bid them strike.
Lead them or follow them in fierce attack
And, spattered with his faithless blood, come back
To claim my grateful heart as your reward.

81

ORESTES

But think, my lady—

HERMIONE

Enough, enough, my lord.
Your quibbling talk offends my righteous ire.
I gave you what Orestes should desire,
A chance to please me; but now I understand:
You'd rather rail at fate than earn my hand.
Go, go, brag elsewhere of your constancy,
And leave the task of my revenge to me.
I've been too kind to you, I blush to say,
And been refused too often in one day.
I'll go to the temple, where soon their rites will start,
And where you dare not act to win my heart.
Alone, I'll seek my enemy out; alone,
I'll pierce the heart I could not make my own.
Then, turning toward my breast the bloody knife,
I'll join our fates in death, if not in life;
And it shall be, though he has proven untrue,
Sweeter to die with him than live with you.

ORESTES

No, I'll deprive you of that dismal joy.
My hand alone shall kill him. I shall destroy
Henceforward, Madam, all your enemies,
And you may thank me for it as you please.

HERMIONE

Go. Trust your fate to me. And do not fail
To have our ships in readiness to sail.

SCENE FOUR

HERMIONE, CLEONE

CLEONE

Madam, you're courting ruin; be aware—

HERMIIONE

What care I? Vengeance is my only care.
I have his promise; but was I wise to ask
Another than myself to do the task?
He feels the guilt of Pyrrhus less than I,
Who could with surer stroke make Pyrrhus die.
What joy to take my own fierce vengeance for
His crime, to stain my arm with traitor's gore,
And, to increase his pain and my delight,
Conceal my rival from his dying sight!
Oh, if at least Orestes lets him know
That in my name he strikes the mortal blow!
Go! Bid him tell the wretch that it's my hate
To which he's sacrificed, and not the state.
Run: unless Pyrrhus knows, when he is slain,
That I'm his slayer, my vengeance will be vain.

CLEONE

I'll do your bidding. But—gods!—how strange a thing!
Who would have thought it, Madam? Here comes the king.

[*Act Four* · *Scene Four*]

HERMIONE

Quick, find Orestes; tell him that before
He acts he must consult with me once more.

SCENE FIVE

PYRRHUS, HERMIONE, PHOENIX

PYRRHUS

Madam, you weren't expecting me; I regret
My interruption of your tête-à-tête.
I haven't come here, full of base pretense,
To cloak my guilty deeds in innocence;
My conscience tells me I am wrong, and I
Have not the art to brazen out a lie.
I take a Trojan wife, and give her—yes,
The faith I promised you. That I confess.
Another man might argue that our chains
Were forged by our two fathers on the plains
Of Troy, where, not consulting you or me,
They matched us with each other, lovelessly.
The fact, however, is that I concurred.
My envoys bore to you my sacred word,
Which I had no intent to disavow:
You came with them to Epirus, and though by now
Another's eyes had with their conquering blaze
Forestalled the power of your brilliant gaze,
I did not let that passion shake my will,
But swore I would be faithful to you still:
Your welcome here was queenly; and till this day
I thought my vows could keep my love at bay.
But now love triumphs; through the unkind Fates,
Andromache has enslaved a heart she hates,
And toward the altar, each dragged by each, we move

To pledge, despite ourselves, undying love.
Now then, denounce my treachery. I despise
My conduct, yet cannot wish it otherwise.
Give free rein to your righteous anger, do:
It will, perhaps, ease me as much as you.
Tell me that I am perjured, false, forsworn:
I fear your silence, not your terms of scorn,
For in my breast a thousand tongues will flay
My conscience all the more, the less you say.

HERMIONE

My lord, I'm glad that you can thus dispense
Full justice to yourself, without pretense,
And that, in breaking our most solemn ties,
You give your crime no virtuous disguise.
But why, indeed, should a great conqueror bow
To slavish dictates, and make good his vow?
No, no, all laws are yours to mock and flout,
And it's to boast of that you've sought me out.
No oath or duty binds you. You can seek
At once to love a Trojan, and wed a Greek!
You leave me, take me back, then once more spurn
For Hector's widow, Helen's child. In turn
You crown the princess and the slave, destroy
Troy for the Greeks, and Greece for Hector's boy!
All this bespeaks a free soul, undeterred
By any servile urge to keep his word.
To please your bride, you'd have me, it appears,
Cry *traitor*, *perjurer*, and dissolve in tears.
You've come here to observe my stricken face,
So as to mock my grief in her embrace.
You'd have me chained to her triumphal car;
But no, that's too much nuptial bliss by far.
And why should I denounce you? Are you not
Contented with the bloody fame you've got?
Hector's old father wounded to the death

86

And gasping, at his kinfolks' feet, for breath,
While, in his bosom, your sword is digging still
For one last drop of frozen blood to spill;
Troy set ablaze, and swamped in seas of gore;
Polyxena destroyed by you before
The indignant eyes of all the Grecian host:
What nobler exploits could a hero boast?

PYRRHUS

Yes, in avenging Helen, well I know
To what extremes my anger made me go.
I could reproach you with the blood I've spilt,
Since you're her daughter; but let's be done with guilt.
Thank heaven that your cold indifference
Now shows me that I love without offense.
I've been too torn by scruples. I should have known
Your feelings better, and better searched my own.
By my remorse I have insulted you;
A man not loved can scarcely be untrue.
When did you show me any jealousy?
I feared I'd wrong you; it seems I've set you free.
Our two hearts, Madam, weren't fated to combine.
You did your duty merely, as I did mine:
But as for love, of course, you pledged me none.

HERMIONE

I haven't loved you? What, then, have I done?
I scorned, for your sake, many a prince's hand;
I came here, of myself, to this raw land;
And here I've stayed, despite your crimes, and though
My Greeks were vexed that I indulged you so.
Waiting for you to turn to me once more,
I bade them not to tell what slights I bore;
Duty, I thought, would prompt you to be true
And bring me back the heart that was my due.

I loved you faithless; had you been faithful, how
Much more could I have loved you? Even now,
Hearing you speak the calm, cold words which kill
My hopes, it may be that I love you still.
My lord, if this must be, if Heaven grants
To other eyes than mine a brighter glance,
Marry her; I consent to it; but at least
Make me no witness of that wedding feast.
I speak to you for the last time, it may be:
Wait but one day. Tomorrow you'll be free . . .
You make no answer? Ah, perjurer, it's clear
How you begrudge each moment wasted here.
Impatient for your Trojan love, you balk
At hearing any voice but hers. You talk
With her in spirit; your blank eyes see her face.
I'll not detain you further; leave this place.
Go, swear to her the faith you swore to me;
Go, go, profane the gods' high majesty:
The gods, the just gods will not have forgot
That we were bound once by the selfsame knot.
Take your false heart to the altar; but beware
Lest you should find Hermione waiting there.

SCENE SIX

PYRRHUS, PHOENIX

PHOENIX

My lord, you heard her; don't underestimate
This vengeful woman so consumed with hate.
She has here many friends and followers;
The cause of Hellas is now linked with hers;
Orestes loves her; and could her hand be won—

PYRRHUS

Andromache awaits me. Guard her son.

SCENE ONE

HERMIONE, *alone*

Where am I? What have I done? What must I do?
What clouds my heart? What cleaves my brain in two?
All through this palace, aimlessly I move.
Alas, I know not whether I hate or love.
Oh, with what cruel eyes he took his leave!—
No pity in them, no pretense to grieve.
Was there a moment's pain or mercy shown?
Could I extract from him a single groan?
Dumb to my sighs, unmoved by my dismay,
Did he seem touched by me in any way?
And still I pity him! Worse yet, my heart
Is cowardly enough to take his part!
I tremble at his danger, and though my will
Cries out for vengeance, I forgive him still!
No, I'll not cancel what my anger swore:
Let the man perish! He lives for me no more.
The traitor mocks my stormy rage, and sneers,
Thinking that it will dissipate in tears;
That, weak and wavering, I'll interpose
One arm to shield him from the other's blows.
He fancies that I'll be, as ever, kind.
But no, the wretch has other things in mind:
Triumphant in the temple, he does not give
A thought to whether I'd have him die or live.
The villain leaves that bitter choice to me.
Well, let Orestes act, let Pyrrhus be
Destroyed; he knew to what his treason led,
And forced me, in the end, to wish him dead.
To wish him . . . what? Have I ordered such a thing?
Because I've loved him, must he die? This king
Whose exploits it was my delight of old

93

To hear again, and yet again, retold,
To whom my secret heart was given, in fact,
Long, long before our ill-starred wedding pact—
Can I have come so far, traversing all
These seas and countries, only to plot his fall,
To slay him, murder him? Oh, lest they kill him now—

SCENE TWO

HERMIONE

What have I done, Cleone? Tell me, how
Is Pyrrhus?

CLEONE

　　　　Madam, he's at the summit of
His hopes; no man is prouder, or more in love.
I saw him leading, like a conqueror,
His latest conquest toward the temple door,
His eyes ablaze with joy, as if he were
Drunk with the pleasure of beholding her.
Andromache, through a thousand shouts of joy,
Moves toward the altar brooding still on Troy;
Unstirred by love or hate, she seems as one
Who does resignedly what must be done.

HERMIONE

And could the wretch sustain his swaggering air?
Cleone, did you search his face with care?
Was it serenely happy? Did his glance
Turn sometimes toward this palace, by any chance?
Did you at some point come within his view?
Did he not blush on recognizing you,

95

And so confess his faithlessness, his shame?
Or was he ever brazenly the same?

CLEONE

Madam, he's blind—not only blind to you,
But to his honor and his safety, too.
He thinks of love alone, and does not know
If those who follow him are friend or foe.
He's given his guard to Hector's son, expecting
That no one but the boy could need protecting,
And bidden Phoenix take him to a fort
Far distant from the temple and the court.
The blithe king has no other cares today.

HERMIONE

He'll die, the scoundrel. But what did Orestes say?

CLEONE

He's gone into the temple, with all his men.

HERMIONE

Is he not planning to avenge me, then?

CLEONE

I don't know.

HERMIONE

What, Orestes too? Shall *he*
Betray me?

96

CLEONE

He adores you utterly.
And yet, assailed by scruples, and divided
'Twixt love and honor, his will is undecided.
In Pyrrhus he reveres the crown and throne,
Reveres Achilles' fame and Pyrrhus' own;
He fears the wrath of Greece and of mankind,
But fears still more, he says, a guilty mind.
He would rejoice to bring you Pyrrhus' head,
But the word *murderer* freezes him with dread.
And so he has gone in, uncertain still
Whether he goes to witness or to kill.

HERMIONE

No, he'll not mar the king's triumphal scene;
He'll be most careful not to intervene.
I know what scruples whisper in his ears:
The coward fears to die; that's all he fears.
Oh, think of it! Without a single plea
My mother roused all Greece to set her free;
For ten years, in her cause, she saw a score
Of kings she did not know destroyed in war;
While I—one perjurer's death is all I claim;
I charge a suitor to avenge my shame,
Tell him that by that test I may be won,
Pledge him my hand, and still the deed's not done!
Enough then: I'll requite my wrongs alone.
That temple shall resound with shriek and moan;
Their cursèd wedding rite shall close in grief
And, by the gods, I'll make their union brief.
Maddened, I'll strike out blindly. In that place
All, even Orestes, shall wear Pyrrhus' face.
I'll die; but die avenged at least, nor be
Alone in dying. Someone shall die with me.

SCENE THREE

ORESTES

Madam, your will is done; the die is cast!
False Pyrrhus, at the altar, breathes his last.

HERMIONE

He's dead?

ORESTES

       He's dying; our angry Greeks today
Have in his own blood washed his crimes away.
I'd promised you as much, and though I could not
Without some horror join in such a plot,
I sped to the temple; there our Greeks had long
Since slipped into the forefront of the throng.
Pyrrhus observed me, and he seemed to be
Moved by my presence to audacity,
As if to flout the Greeks' ambassador
Might make his brilliant marriage shine the more.
He took the diadem, set it on the head
Of his Andromache and, exulting, said,
"My crown, my troth are yours, Andromache;
Be queen of all Epirus and of me.
I promise to your son a father's care;
Let the gods witness what I gladly swear.

His enemies I make my own; the boy
I recognize and hail as king of Troy."
Hearing these words, which pleased the people well,
Our Greeks responded with a wrathful yell.
At once they ringed the traitor round. I drew
My sword to strike him, but could not get through.
Each vied with each to hew him down, and I
Beheld his bloody struggles, saw him try
To dodge their strokes, so many and so fast,
Till by the altar he collapsed at last.
Then, through the crowd's affrighted turbulence,
I passed, in haste to bear my princess hence
And gain the port, where soon our friends are due,
All spattered with the blood I promised you.

HERMIONE

What have they done?

ORESTES

                    Forgive their haste. I see
That they've betrayed your vengeance. You wanted me
To be the first to strike, and him to know
That it was in your cause I struck the blow.
Yet, Madam, it was my zeal that fanned their flame:
I led them to the temple in your name
Alone, and you may rightly claim a kill
In which they were but agents of your will.
'Twas you whose blows—

HERMIONE

                    Hush, liar. Don't seek to hide
The guilt you bear for this vile regicide.
Go boast of it in Greece. I disavow
Your craven butchery. Go! I abhor you now.

99

Barbarian! What have you done? How mad a crime
To cut down such a being in his prime!
How could your men kill such a one as he
And all their blood not rise in mutiny?
But speak: who gave you power to judge his lot?
By what right did you murder him, and for what?
Who told you to?

ORESTES

What? Gods! Did you not ordain
Here in this place, just now, that he be slain?

HERMIONE

Ah, why believe a love-crazed woman? Could
You not divine where inwardly I stood?
In all my ravings, could you not discern
How my heart belied my lips at every turn?
Even if I'd meant it, had you to assent?
Oughtn't you to have questioned my intent
A hundred times, come back to urge delay
And caution, or still better, stayed away?
Why couldn't you leave my vengeance up to me?
Why did you come here, you whom I'd sought to flee?
Look how your love's borne fruit in blood and wrath:
You've brought to me the doom that dogs your path.
But for your fatal mission, which chafed his will
And made him choose my rival, Pyrrhus would still
Have portioned out his heart between us two;
Loved me, perhaps; at least, pretended to.
Go. You may leave now. I shall stay here alone,
Renouncing Greece, and Sparta, and its throne,
And all my people, whom I regard with scorn,
Since from their loins a beast like you was born.

SCENE FOUR

ORESTES, *alone*

Was this Hermione? What were those things she said?
For whom, then, flows the blood which I have shed?
I am a murderer, if her words be true.
Am I Orestes? Is it Pyrrhus who
Has died? Great gods! I thwart my conscience, bring
Myself to butcher an anointed king,
At one stroke breaking all the laws designed
By Heaven for monarchs, envoys, and mankind,
Defiling too the altar where he died;
For whom do I commit this regicide
And sacrilege? A thankless woman, who swore
That I must do it, or see her face no more,
Whose rage I made my own. Her foe once slain,
She bids me bring him back to life again!
She loves him! I am a brute, a beast, she cries,
And, fleeing now forever from my eyes,
The one reward she gives me is to confer
The hateful names I earned by serving her.

SCENE FIVE

PYLADES

My lord, it's time we went. Unless we do,
We shan't get out alive, I promise you.
Our Greeks can't hold the palace gates for long
Against an irate people, armed and strong.
This land is ruled now by Andromache;
She is its queen, and we its enemy.
She, once averse to Pyrrhus, plays the part
Of faithful widow now with all her heart,
Demands revenge for him, and may pursue
Vengeance on us for Troy and Hector too.
Let's leave, Sir, lest we fall into their hands;
Our men will follow us; while the crowd still stands
Around Hermione in the square below,
Our way is clear, and we may safely go.

ORESTES

No, it's Hermione I shall follow, friends:
She has condemned me; here my story ends.
Go, go. My crime must have its punishment.

PYLADES

Forget Hermione, Sir. As instrument
And victim of her fury, must you go

And seek new wrongs among the shades below?
Because she's dying, must you die with her?

ORESTES

She's dying? O gods!

PYLADES

Did you not know it, Sir?
As we were coming back, Hermione passed
Us, running toward the temple, all aghast.
She met with Pyrrhus, borne by soldiers whom
His blood made furious to avenge his doom.
The sight no doubt deranged her. We could see
From the palace gate how, armed with a dagger, she
Bent over Pyrrhus—then, terrible to tell,
Looked up to heaven, stabbed herself, and fell.

ORESTES

The gods be thanked for this unlooked-for woe!
I praise thee, Heaven, for persisting so.
Bent on afflicting me without relief,
Thou hast upraised me to the heights of grief.
Thy hatred has rejoiced to make me mourn;
'Twas to display thy wrath that I was born,
And be misfortune's pure embodiment.
Well then, my fate's fulfilled; I die content.
Where are these lovers? My bliss shall not be crowned
Till, in their blood and mine, I shall be drowned.
I want to hold them in my dying sight,
Joining three hearts that life could not unite.
But what's this thick and sudden darkness? How
Shall I get out of it? Why do I shudder now?

What shakes my bones? Thank heaven, my eyes grow
   clear . . .
O gods! What streams of blood rush round me here!

PYLADES

My lord—

ORESTES

      What! Pyrrhus, do we meet once more?
Can't I escape this rival I abhor?
How did you get away, pierced through and through?
Well, here's the thrust that I have saved for you.
But what is this I see? Hermione throws
Her arms about him to avert my blows.
Gods! How her fiery glances make me quake!
What are these fiends and serpents in her wake?
I know now: daughters of Hades, are you there?
For whom these hissing serpents in your hair,
And all these presences of pain and fright?
D'you come to drag me into endless night?
Then come: I shall embrace your cruelty.
No. Stand back. Leave me to Hermione:
Better than you she tears her prey apart;
Let her at last devour my proffered heart.

PYLADES

His senses leave him. Friends, we must not waste
The time this seizure grants us. Come, make haste
And save him. If he wakens here again
Still frenzied, all our efforts will be vain.